ARCHAEOLOGY FOR KIDS ASIA

TOP ARCHAEOLOGICAL DIG SITES AND DISCOVERIES

GUIDE ON ARCHAEOLOGICAL ARTIFACTS

5TH GRADE SOCIAL STUDIES

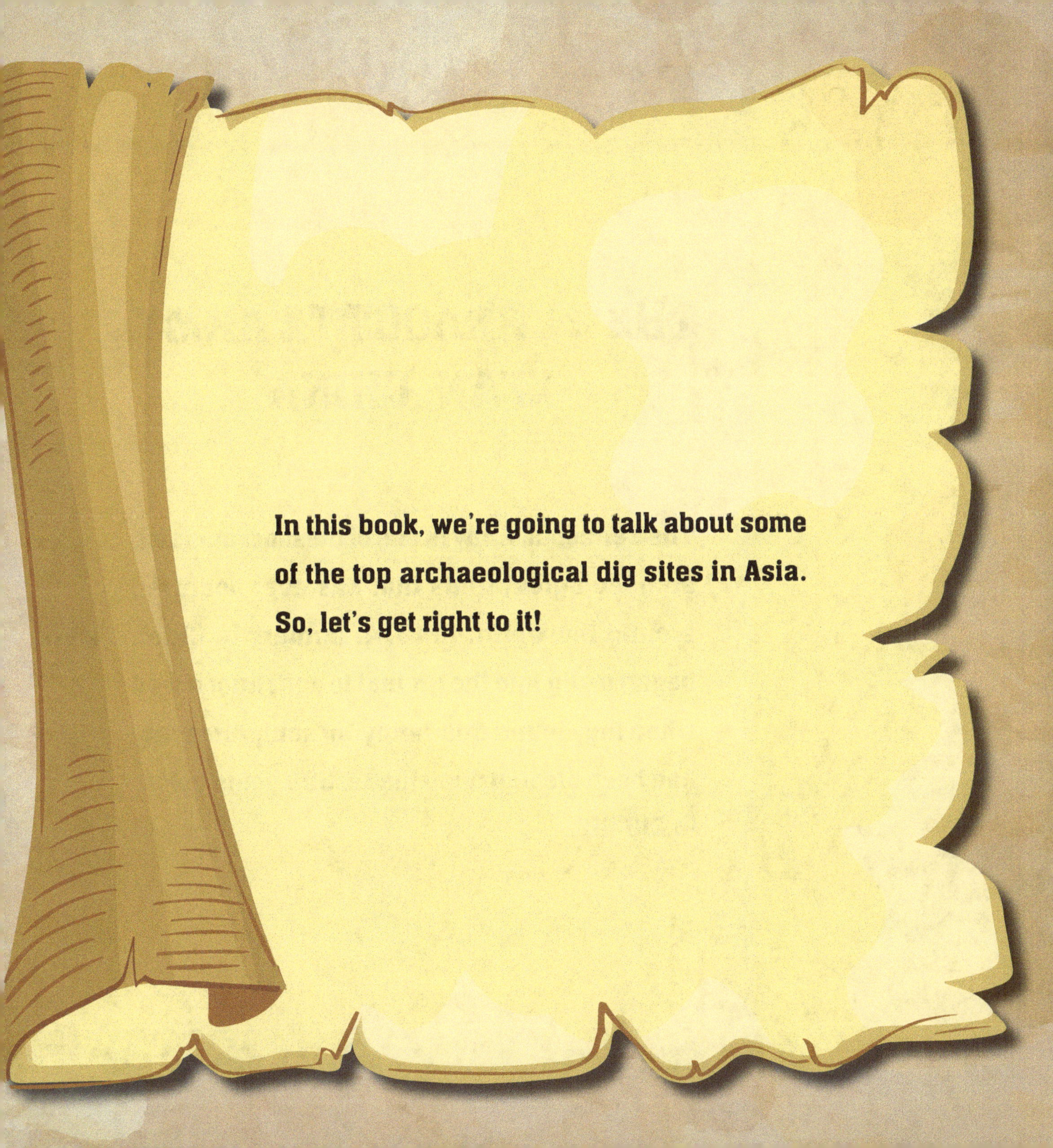
In this book, we're going to talk about some
of the top archaeological dig sites in Asia.
So, let's get right to it!

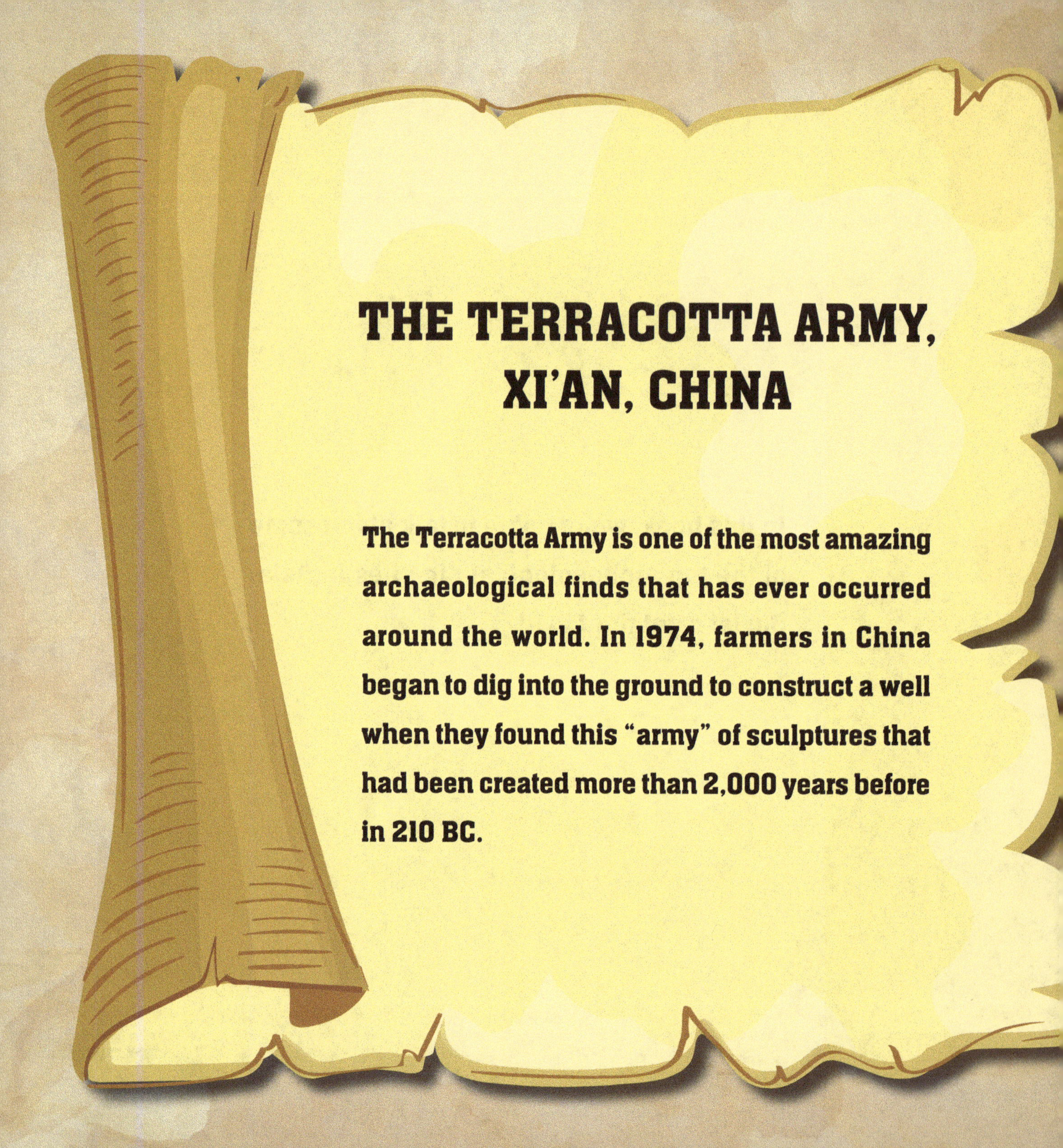

THE TERRACOTTA ARMY, XI'AN, CHINA

The Terracotta Army is one of the most amazing archaeological finds that has ever occurred around the world. In 1974, farmers in China began to dig into the ground to construct a well when they found this "army" of sculptures that had been created more than 2,000 years before in 210 BC.

The artifacts that they found are part of an enormous tomb that was built for Emperor Qin Shi Huang, who was the first emperor of China and who also started the construction of China's Great Wall.

It is the largest burial complex that has ever been found. The "army" was designed to provide security for the emperor in the afterlife.

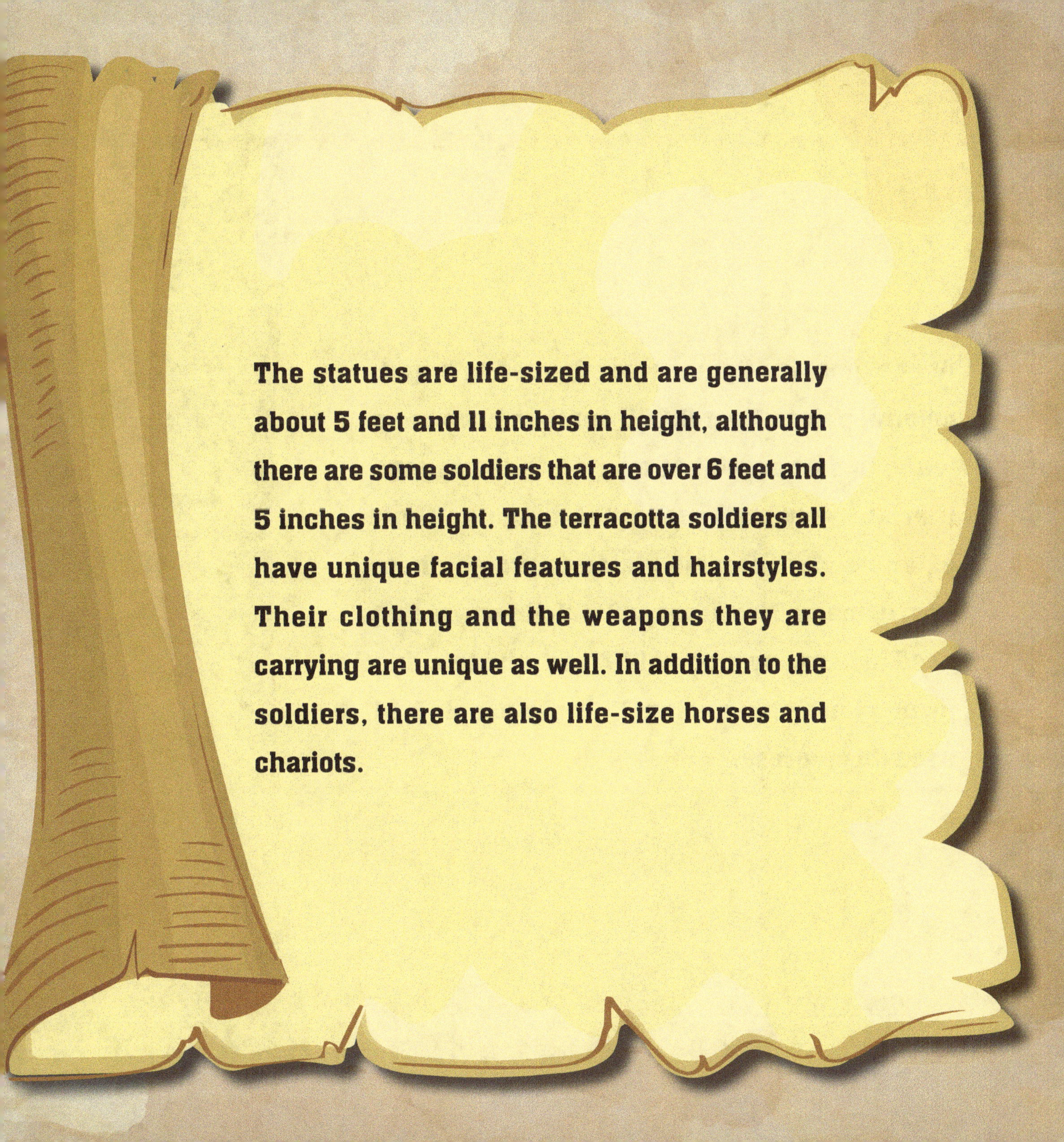

The statues are life-sized and are generally about 5 feet and 11 inches in height, although there are some soldiers that are over 6 feet and 5 inches in height. The terracotta soldiers all have unique facial features and hairstyles. Their clothing and the weapons they are carrying are unique as well. In addition to the soldiers, there are also life-size horses and chariots.

At one time, the figures were painted in bright, colorful paints. Over 8,000 soldiers have been found to date as well as over 40,000 weapons that are very well preserved because their exteriors were chrome plated to protect them from damage. This advanced technique was first used in Germany around 1937, so until this find no one knew that ancient Chinese people had used this process.

Archaeological work is continuing at the site. Less than 1% of the massive tomb has been excavated even though it has been over 40 years since it was found. Although archaeologists want to dig into the tomb, there are some very real safety concerns.

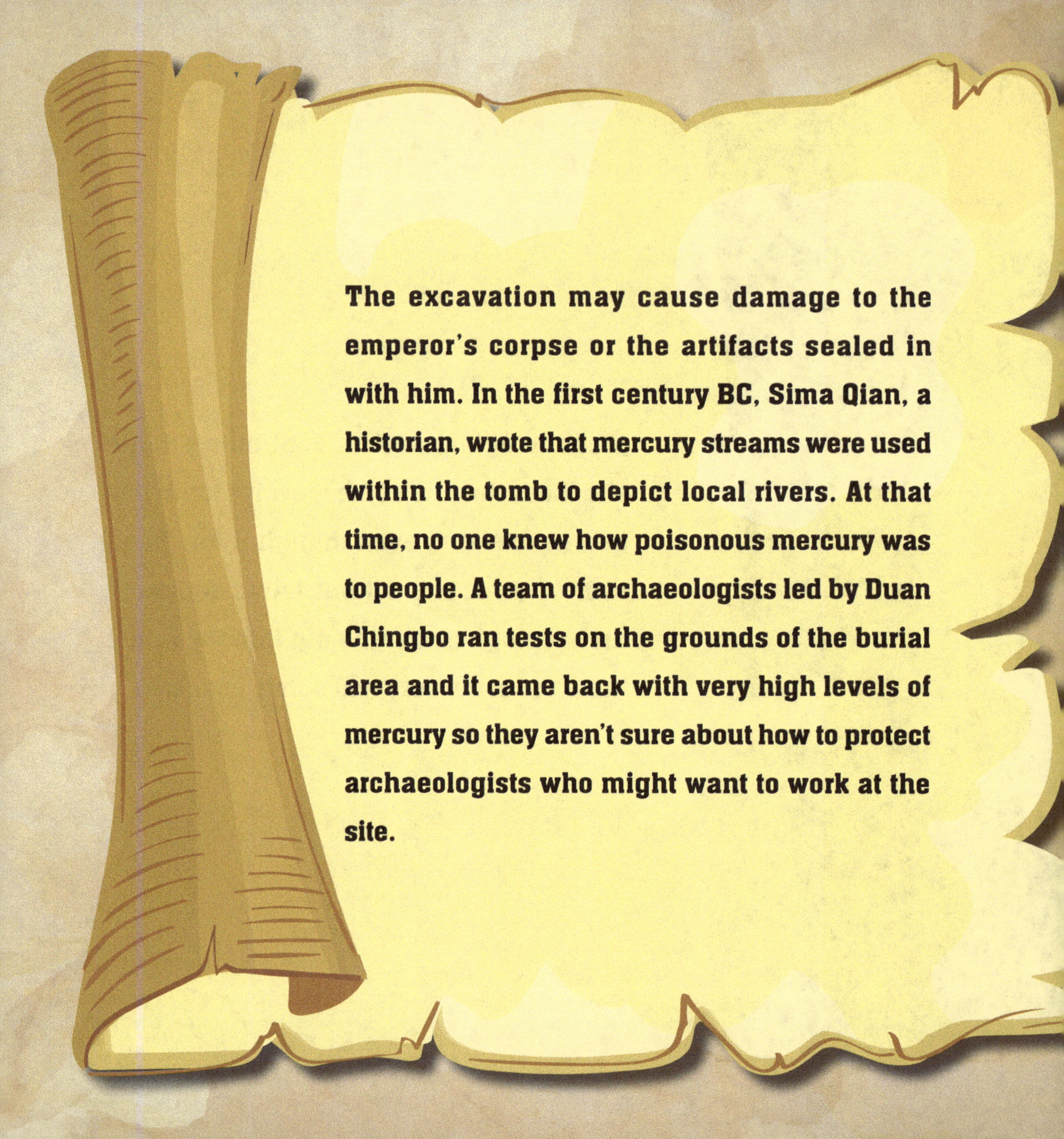

The excavation may cause damage to the emperor's corpse or the artifacts sealed in with him. In the first century BC, Sima Qian, a historian, wrote that mercury streams were used within the tomb to depict local rivers. At that time, no one knew how poisonous mercury was to people. A team of archaeologists led by Duan Chingbo ran tests on the grounds of the burial area and it came back with very high levels of mercury so they aren't sure about how to protect archaeologists who might want to work at the site.

AYUTTHAYA HISTORICAL PARK

AYUTTHAYA, THAILAND

About 85 kilometers north of the city of Bangkok, the city of Ayutthaya stands in the central plains region of Thailand. Still populated today, the city has ancient ruins from many centuries ago when it was at its height.

In foreign countries, the Kingdom of Ayutthaya was called "Siam," but the people who lived there described it as the "Tai Kingdom." It was established in 1350 AD and became the kingdom's second capital city after the capital was moved from Sukhothai.

AYUTTHAYA

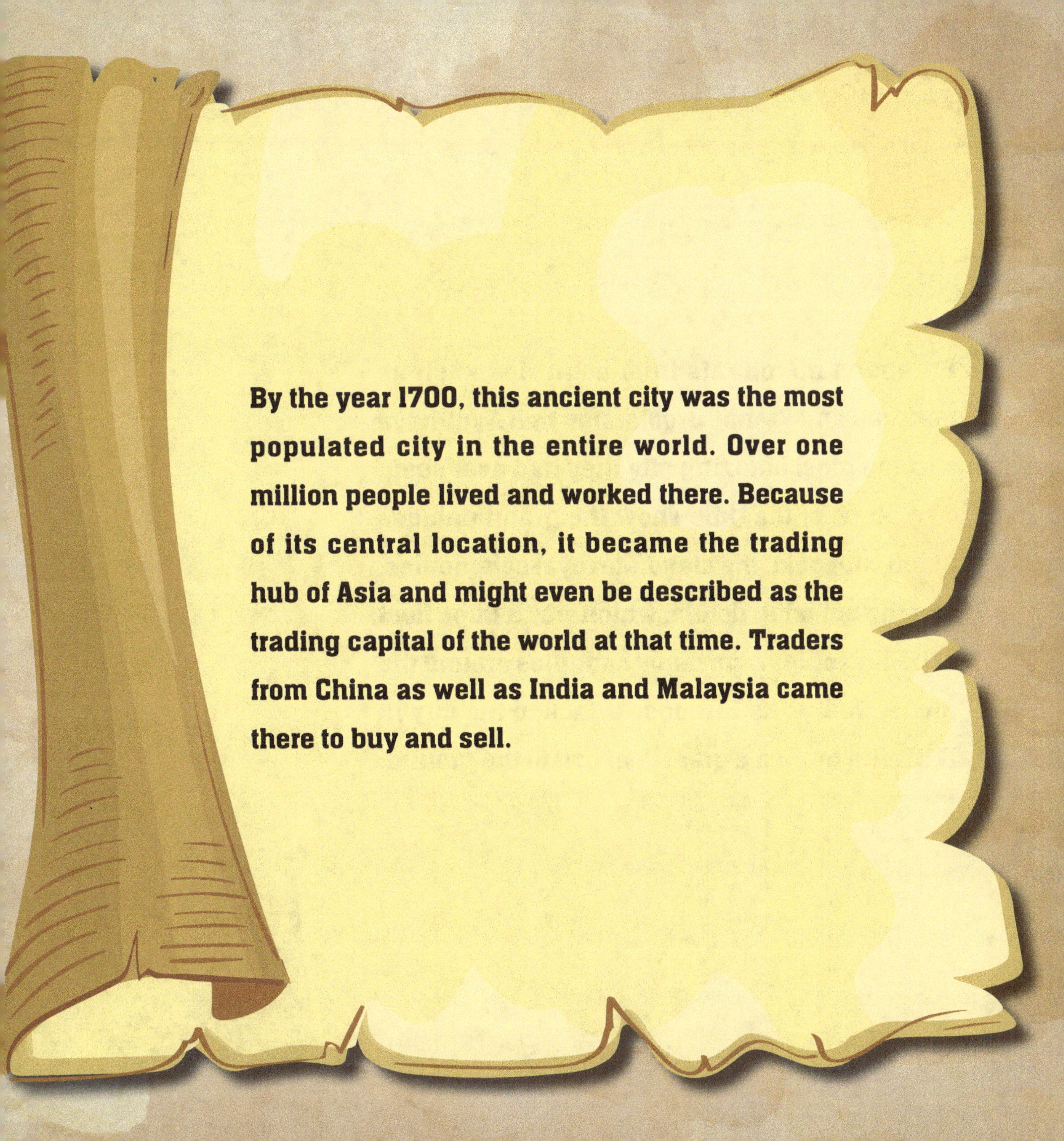

By the year 1700, this ancient city was the most populated city in the entire world. Over one million people lived and worked there. Because of its central location, it became the trading hub of Asia and might even be described as the trading capital of the world at that time. Traders from China as well as India and Malaysia came there to buy and sell.

European merchants from countries such as Portugal and France proclaimed that Ayutthaya was the most amazing city they had ever seen. The maps of the time show the grand palaces laden with gold, the elaborate royal ceremonies, and the amazing flotilla, which was a huge fleet of trading ships from many countries around the globe. Sadly, the Burmese attacked the city in 1767 and burned a great deal of it to the ground.

The remains that are left give an impression of the beautiful city that was once there. Stone buildings, primarily temples as well as palaces and monasteries, are the ruins that are left from the city's former grandeur. At one time, the city had more than 400 Buddhist monasteries. Some of the buildings have distinctive sanctuary towers called prangs. Archaeological excavations began in 1969 and are still ongoing.

AJANTA CAVES, INDIA

In 1819, John Smith, a cavalry soldier from Britain was hunting for a tiger when he noticed a cave above the Waghora River in India, located in the state of Maharashtra. He could tell that the cave had been manmade. He went into the cave with a torch and inside he gazed in wonder at a huge vaulted hall with beautiful, yet faded, paintings on the walls.

AJANTA

AJANTA CAVES

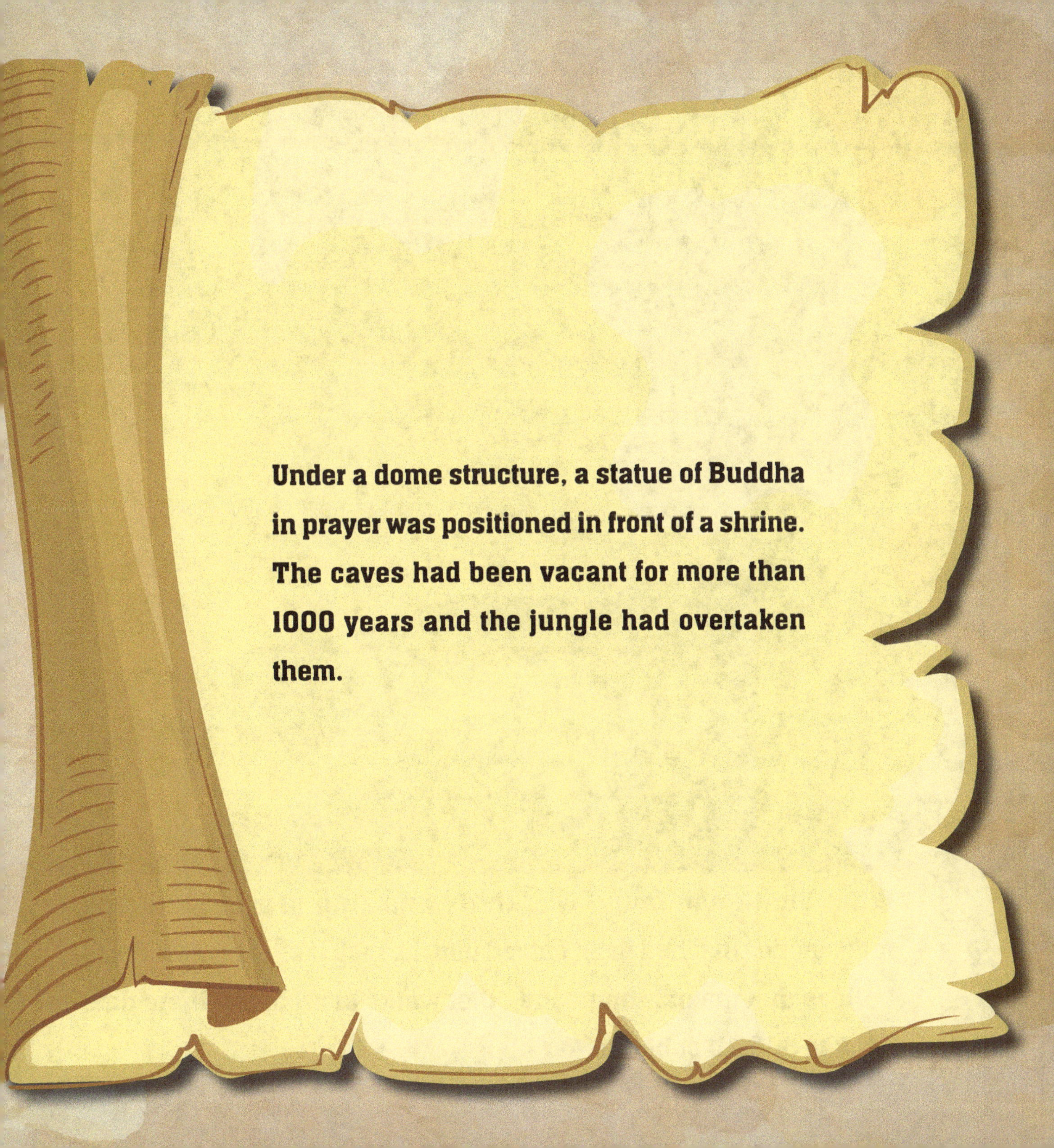

Under a dome structure, a statue of Buddha in prayer was positioned in front of a shrine. The caves had been vacant for more than 1000 years and the jungle had overtaken them.

What Smith had found was thirty amazing prayer halls and monasteries that had been carved into the rock face. Archaeologists believe that the paintings and other works of art found there date back to 500 AD or before.

The caves are essentially a gallery of some of the most beautiful Buddhist art that has ever been discovered including a serene sleeping Buddha.

AJANTA CAVES PAINTING

Some of the paintings were influenced by Greek art, since by that time Alexander the Great had conquered vast areas of Europe and Asia. The paintings depict religious images but they also depict princes, princesses clothed in silks and jewelry, animals, and scenes of royal life.

Beginning in 1991, an archaeological team led by Rajdeo Singh has worked to reveal the original intense color pigments and beauty of the works of art using new restoration methods that were developed in Japan. Their work has led to new questions since no one knows how the original artists could have created such amazing work on the inside of dark caves.

AJANTA CAVES PAINTING

PETRA, JORDAN

In the early 1800s, a traveler from Europe disguised himself by wearing the clothing of a Bedouin so he could go into the mysterious area now known as the ruins of the city of Petra.

This prehistoric city in Jordan was carved into a pink sandstone cliff. Between 400 BC and 106 AD, the now-abandoned city was the capital of a thriving trade center called the Nabataean kingdom.

The city became famous when the entrance to its Treasury, called Al Khazneh, was used as a model for a scene in the movie Indiana Jones. However, the movie didn't show factual details since the Treasury is not very deep once you enter. It is a small hall once used as a tomb for royals. There are dozens of other tombs and other structures carved within the rocks at Petra.

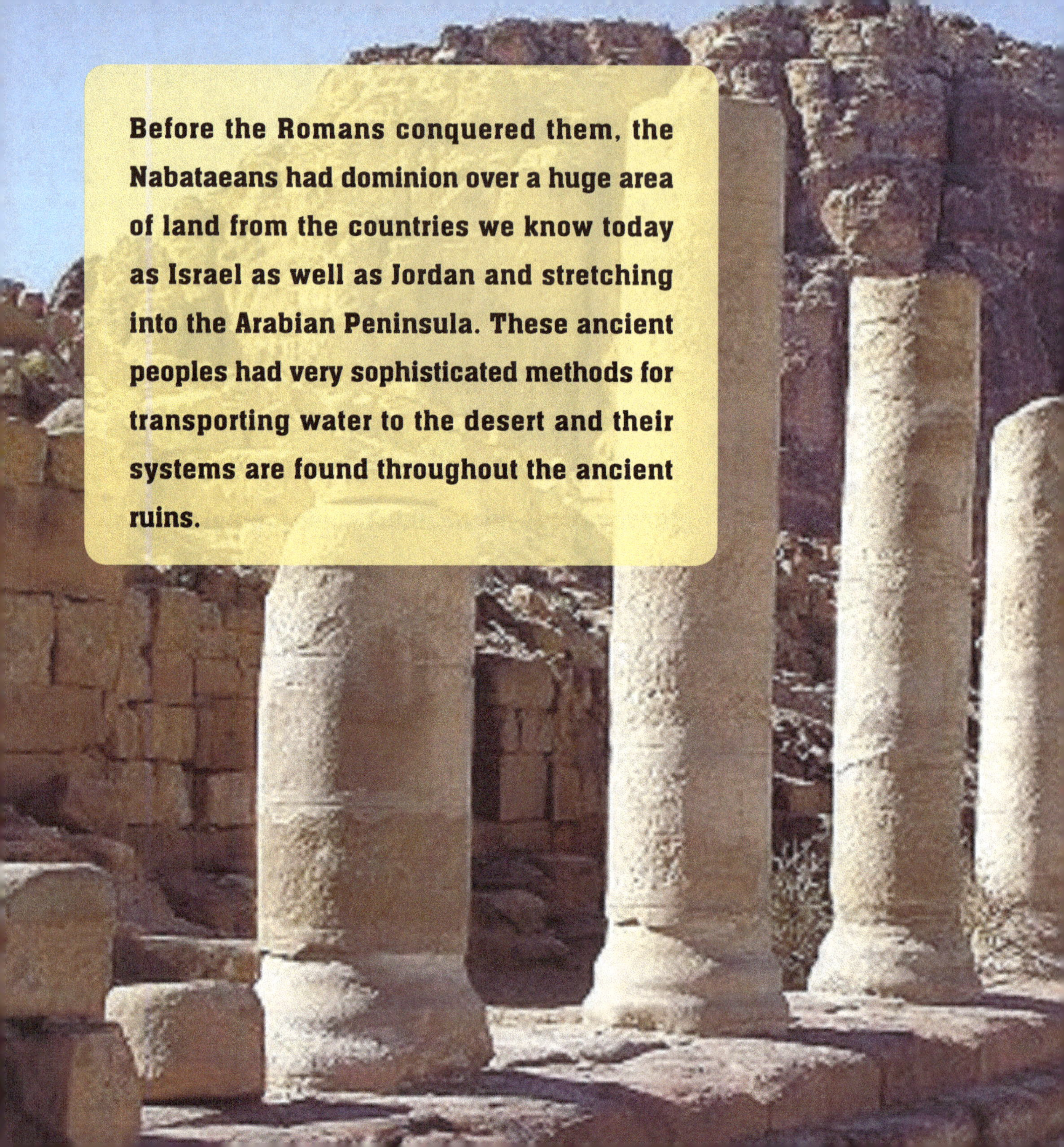
Before the Romans conquered them, the Nabataeans had dominion over a huge area of land from the countries we know today as Israel as well as Jordan and stretching into the Arabian Peninsula. These ancient peoples had very sophisticated methods for transporting water to the desert and their systems are found throughout the ancient ruins.

Al-Muheisen, an archaeologist from Yarmouk University in Jordan, has been excavating the area along with his team beginning in 1979. Their digs have uncovered artifacts from the first century BC. It takes many years to excavate an area as large as Petra. At this point, as much as 80 percent or more of the city is still underground.

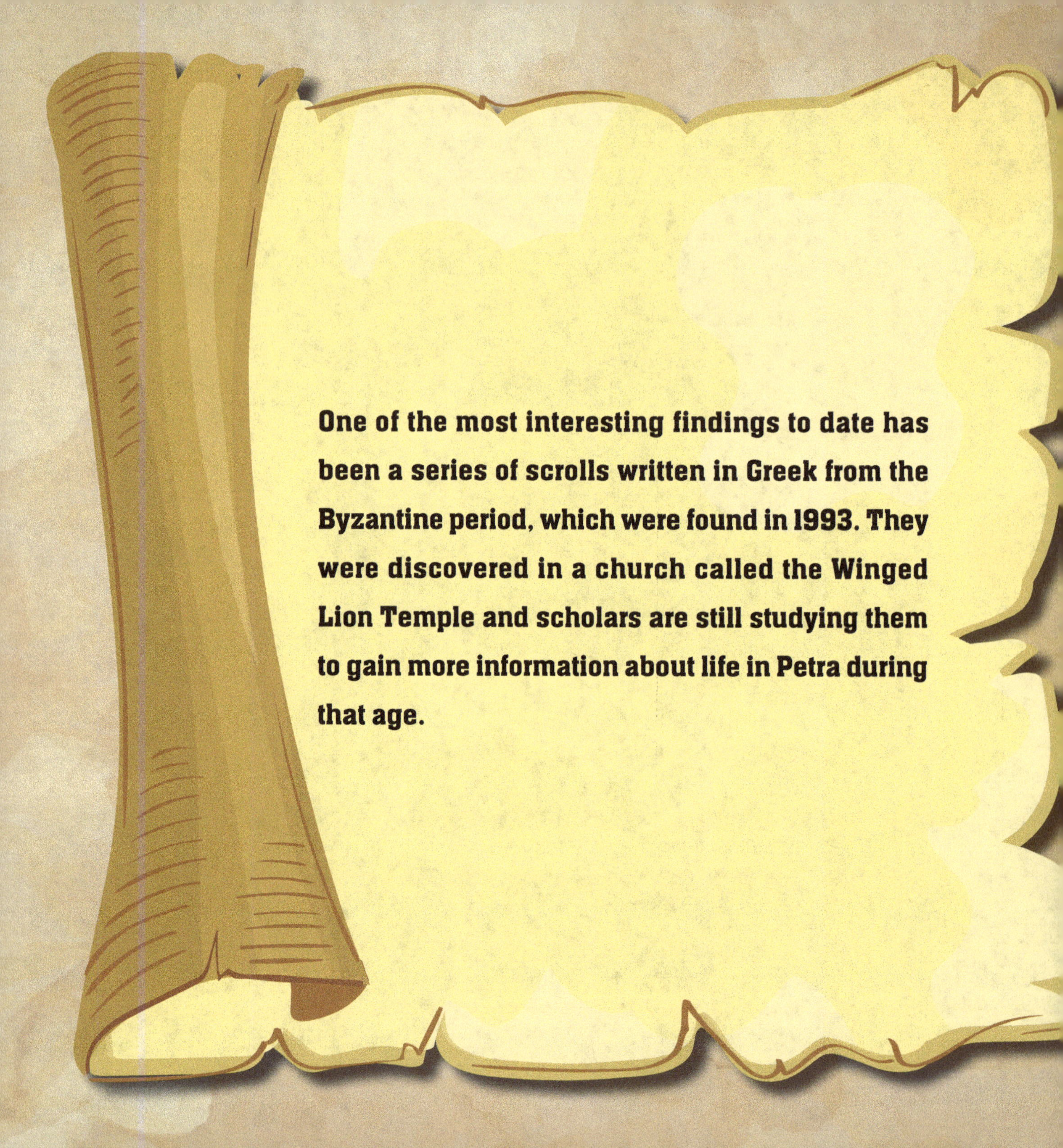

One of the most interesting findings to date has been a series of scrolls written in Greek from the Byzantine period, which were found in 1993. They were discovered in a church called the Winged Lion Temple and scholars are still studying them to gain more information about life in Petra during that age.

VTINAM
MAIORA
AVSVRI
81

CHINA'S GREAT WALL

During the Qin Dynasty, the first emperor of a unified China was Emperor Qin Shi Huang.

He began the construction of an enormous wall designed to keep out the invading Mongols at the country's northern border.

Over a period of more than 1,000 years, subsequent dynasties
continued work on the wall until it was over 5,000 miles along.

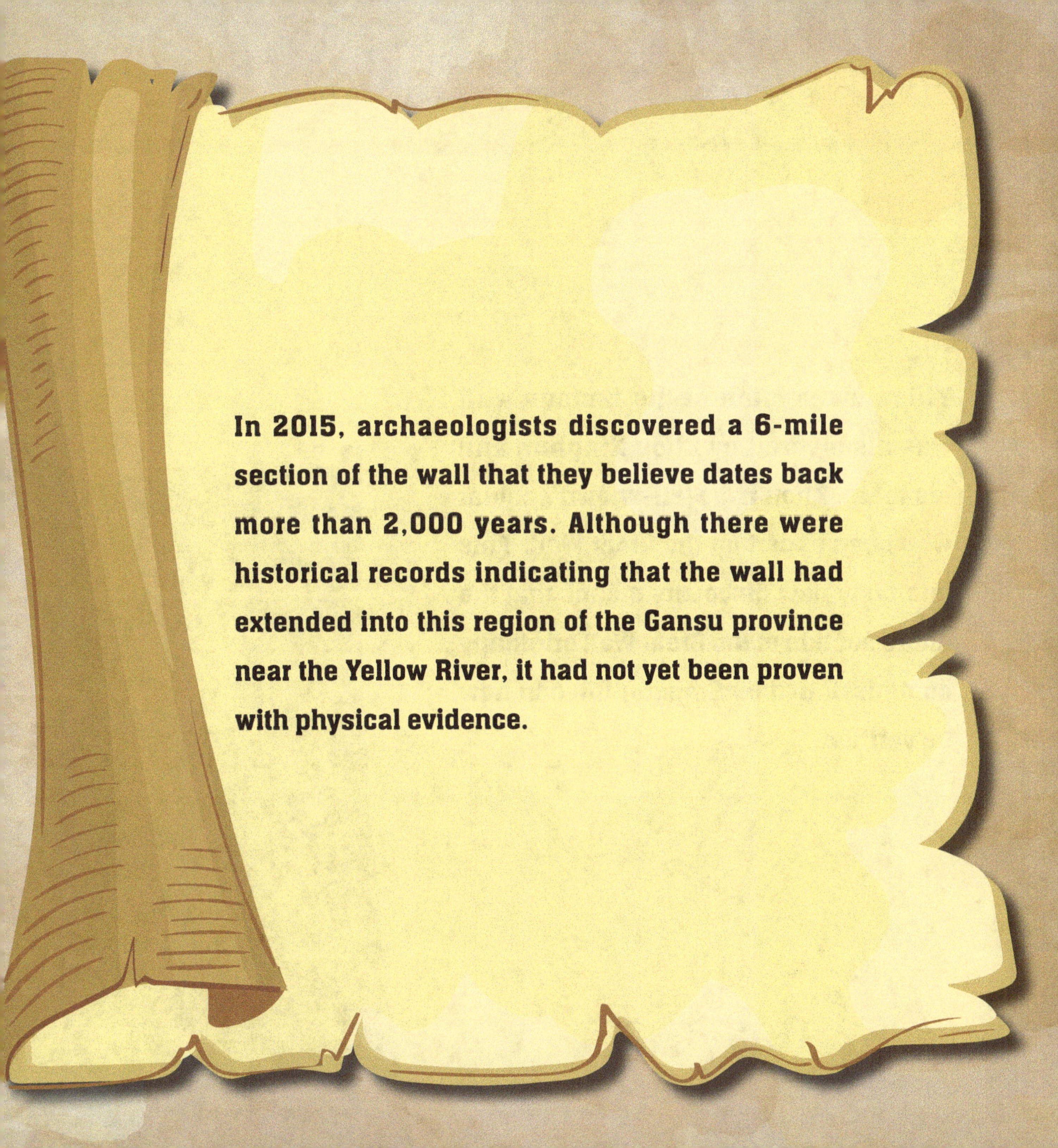

In 2015, archaeologists discovered a 6-mile section of the wall that they believe dates back more than 2,000 years. Although there were historical records indicating that the wall had extended into this region of the Gansu province near the Yellow River, it had not yet been proven with physical evidence.

This new section of the famous wall was discovered by Zhou Xinghua and his team. Zhou is a well-known scholar who is an expert on the Great Wall. This relatively new discovery means that the entire section of the Great Wall originally commissioned by Emperor Qin can now be verified.

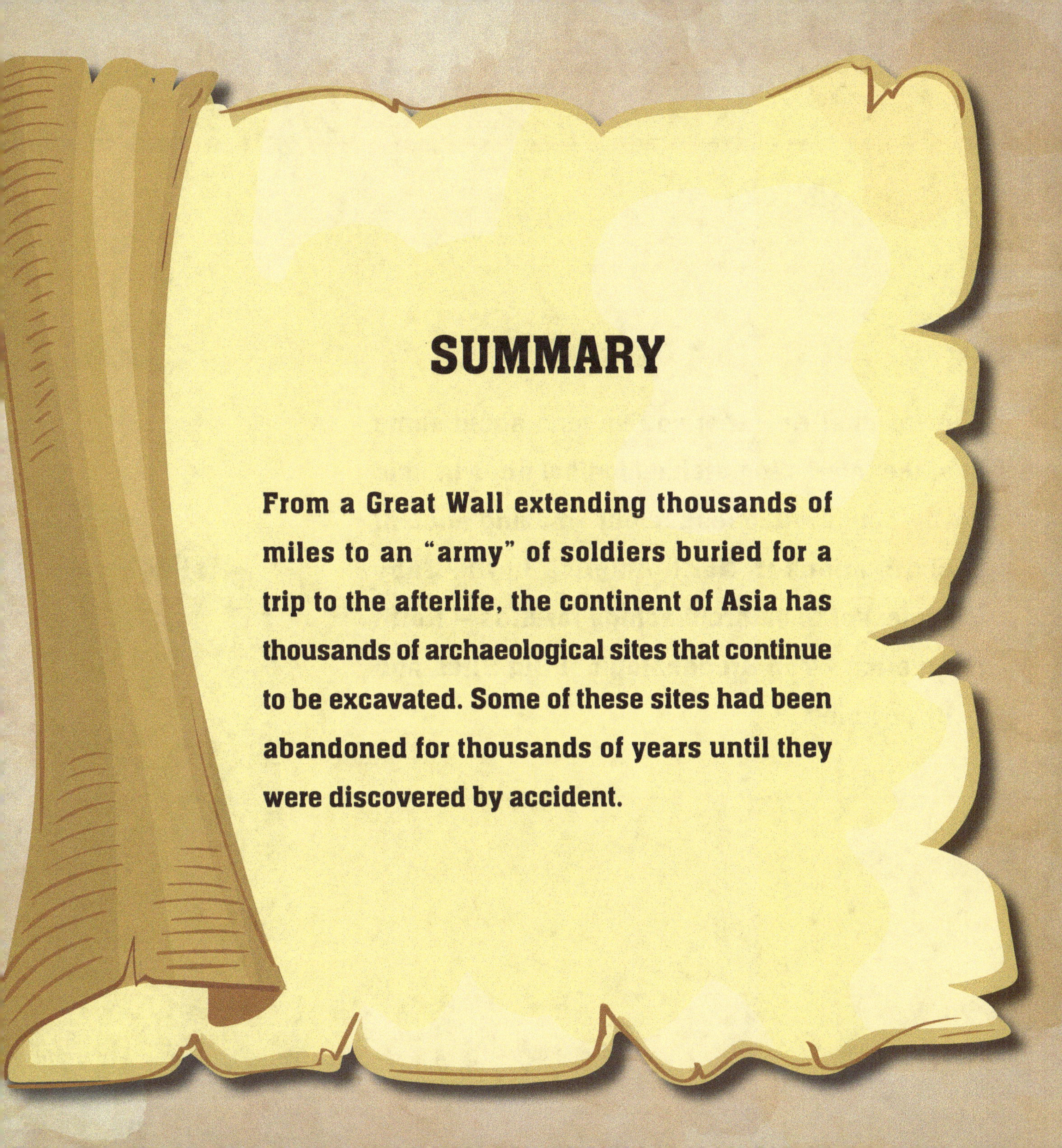

SUMMARY

From a Great Wall extending thousands of miles to an "army" of soldiers buried for a trip to the afterlife, the continent of Asia has thousands of archaeological sites that continue to be excavated. Some of these sites had been abandoned for thousands of years until they were discovered by accident.

Awesome! Now that you've read about some of the interesting archaeological finds in Asia you may want to read about amazing ancient civilizations in North America in the Baby Professor book Archaeology for Kids – North America –Top Archaeological Dig Sites and Discoveries.

Visit

BABY PROFESSOR
EDUCATION KIDS

www.BabyProfessorBooks.com
to download Free Baby Professor eBooks
and view our catalog of new and exciting
Children's Books

9 798869 436245